Investigating Plate Tectonics

Greg Young, M.S.Ed.

Earth and Space Science Readers:
Investigating Plate Tectonics

Publishing Credits

Editorial Director
Dona Herweck Rice

Associate Editor
Joshua BishopRoby

Editor-in-Chief
Sharon Coan, M.S.Ed.

Creative Director
Lee Aucoin

Illustration Manager
Timothy J. Bradley

Publisher
Rachelle Cracchiolo, M.S.Ed.

Science Contributor
Sally Ride Science

Science Consultants
Nancy McKeown,
Planetary Geologist
William B. Rice,
Engineering Geologist

Teacher Created Materials
5301 Oceanus Drive
Huntington Beach, CA 92649-1030
http://www.tcmpub.com

ISBN 978-0-7439-0559-6

Printed by: 51497
Printed in: China

Table of Contents

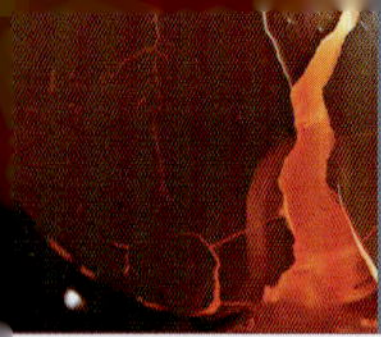

Earth's Crust

Imagine Earth as a hard-boiled egg. An egg has a shell. Earth has a crust. An egg has liquid under its shell. Earth has hot **magma** under its crust. If the Earth were an egg, it would be a 6,400-kilometer (4,000-mile) trip from its shell (the crust) down to its center!

We live on Earth's crust. The crust is the part of Earth that has cooled and hardened. All of the **continents** of Earth are a part of the crust. The ocean floor is also a part of the crust. Mountains rise up from the crust. And just like an eggshell with a crack, our crust is cracked. If you look at the edges of the continents, you might notice that they look like cracks on an eggshell.

Earth also has other layers beneath the crust. They are the mantle and the outer and inner core.

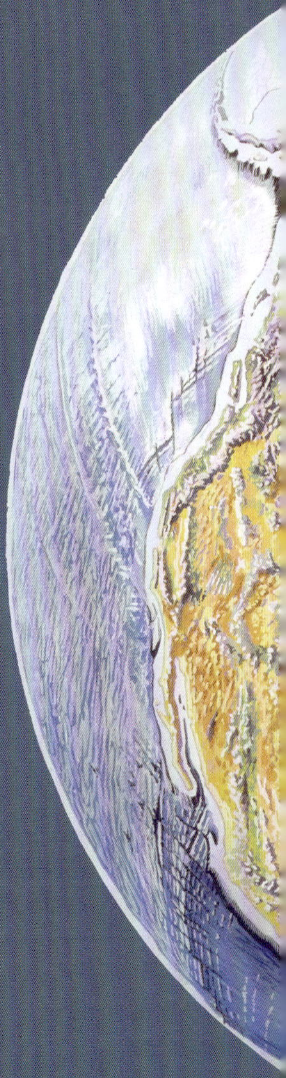

When magma oozes out of the earth's crust, it is called lava.

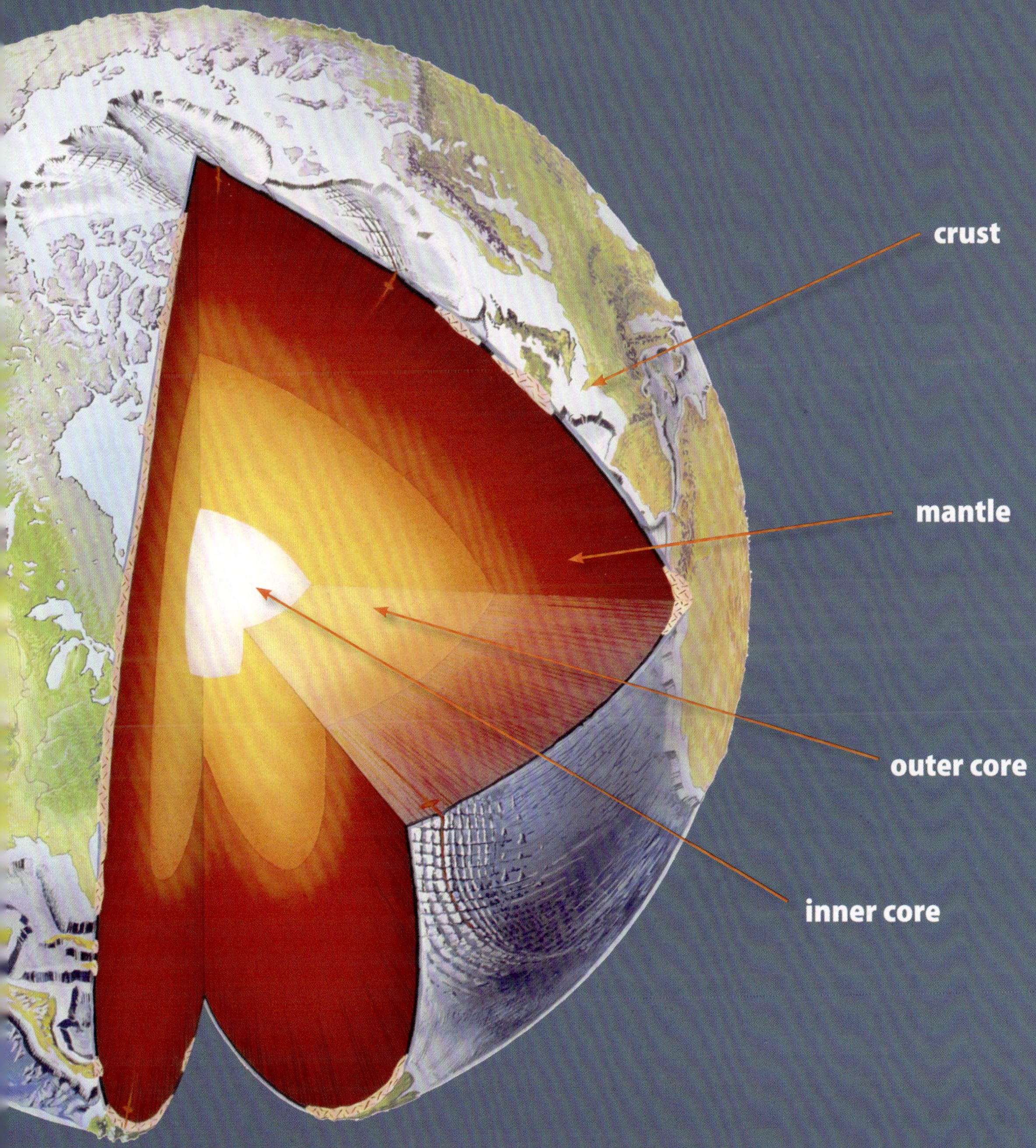

In this diagram, sections of the earth have been removed to show its internal structure.

Underwater Adventures

Carol Hirozawa Reiss is a **marine geologist** (earth scientist who studies oceans) for the U.S. government. She has taken two plunges to the ocean floor in a **submersible** vehicle. A submersible vehicle can travel underwater. On these dives, Reiss worked as a scientific observer. She took careful notes of the strange creatures she saw lurking in the ocean depths. Reiss also worked with equipment that measured how fast the ocean plates on the sea floor are spreading apart.

Tube worms feeding at base of a black smoker chimney hydrothermal vent

JOHNSON-SEA-LINK's six-inch-thick acrylic sphere holds a pilot and an observer.

In 1915, a scientist named Alfred Wegener said that the continents used to be together. Earth once had a huge single landmass. Wegener was not the first scientist to think this. But he was the first to try to show that the shapes of the continents were not just a **coincidence**. He used the clues of Earth's crust to support his **theory**. His theory was known as **continental drift**. It led to the study of **plate tectonics**.

About 200 million years ago, the landmasses of Earth were together. This single landmass was called **Pangea**. We also know that the hot, molten magma under the surface of the crust pushed the lands apart. And this motion continues today!

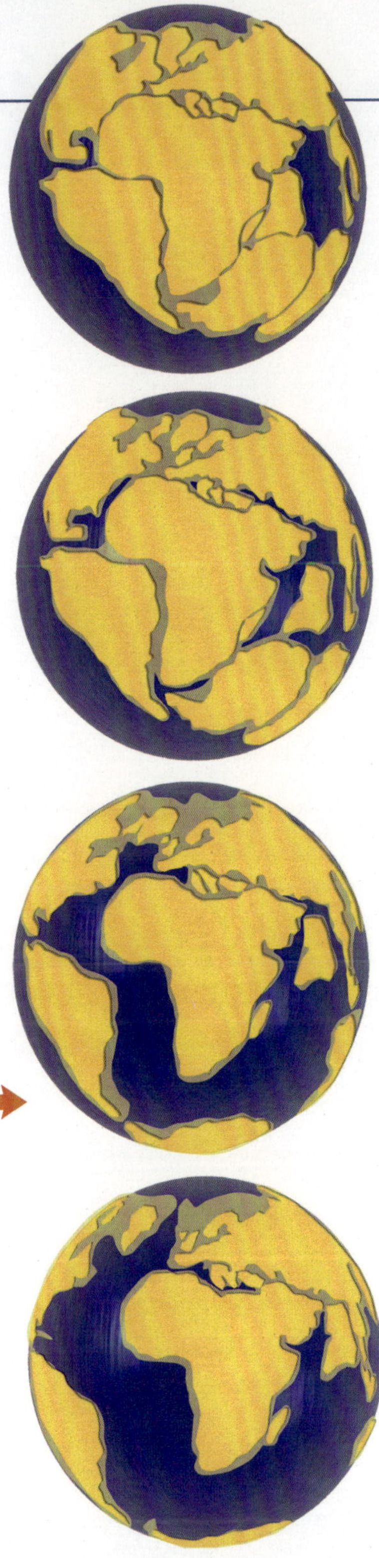

Throughout its history, Earth's landmasses have come together and broken apart many times.

Fun Fact

Earth is very hot inside. There are several reasons for this. For example, heat comes from the radioactive elements. It also comes from friction as the tectonic plates grind against each other. The core temperature of Earth is hotter than the surface of the sun!

Evidence of Plate Tectonics

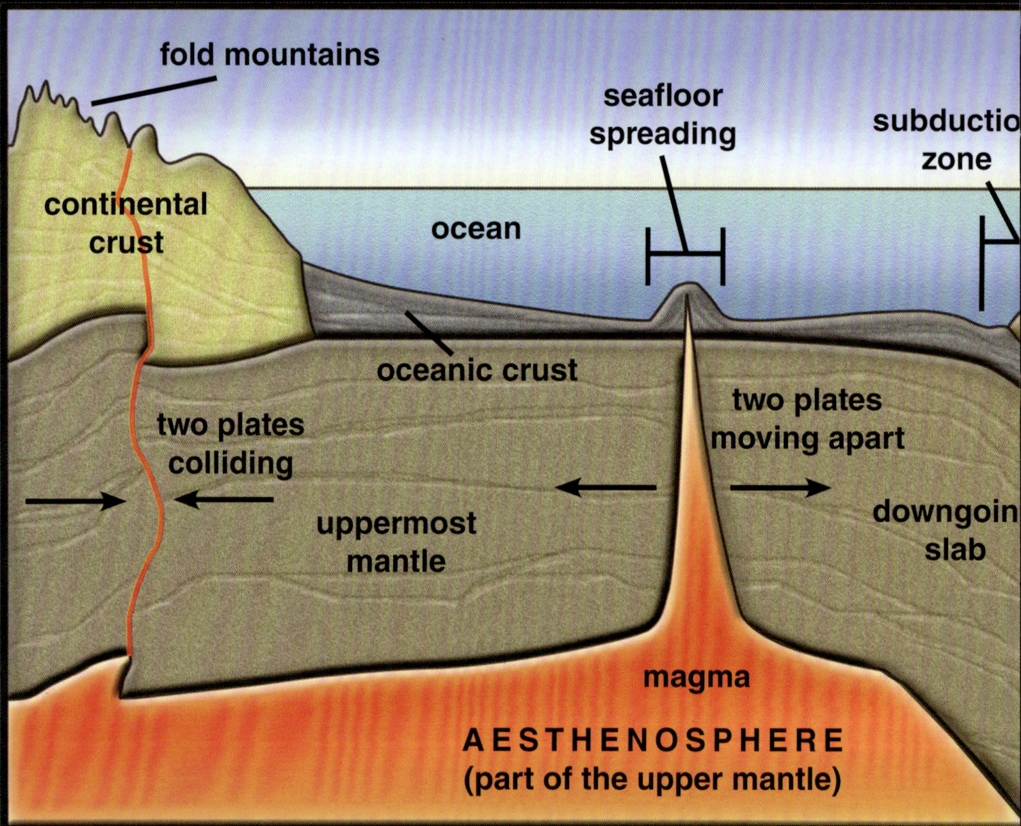

Many geologists did not accept plate tectonics at first. They could see that some continents looked like they could fit together. Most scientists thought this was a coincidence.

Alfred Wegener needed to explain how the continents moved. He said two forces caused the movement. They are the pull of the moon on Earth and the daily spin of Earth itself. Most geologists thought these forces were too weak to move the giant continents.

Wegener did not live long enough to find the reason for continental movement. He died in 1930.

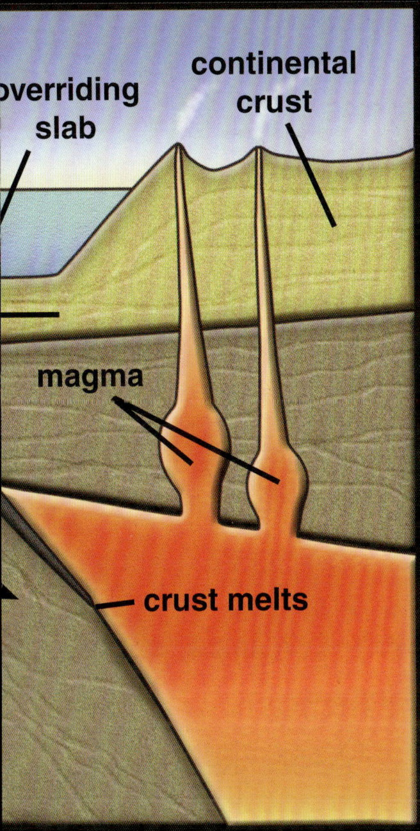

Plate tectonics has many effects all across the world.

During the 40 years after his death, scientists learned more about Earth's crust. Using special tools, geologists mapped the seafloor. They discovered areas such as the **mid-ocean ridge**. The mid-ocean ridge is more than a 50,000 kilometer (31,000 mile) crack in the ocean's floor. It runs from the Arctic down through the Atlantic Ocean. It then circles the globe like the seam of a baseball. Finally, a method to explain how continents move was taking shape!

How Low Can You Go?

The deepest hole ever dug into Earth's crust is only 12 kilometers (7.5 miles).

Another Missing Piece

After Wegener's death, scientists noticed mountains and deep trenches underneath the Pacific Ocean. These discoveries were the missing pieces that Wegener was looking for. They helped to explain plate movement. Magma was pushing the plates apart at cracks in Earth's crust! Magma is in motion. The plates of crust rest on the surface of the moving magma. This causes the plates to move, too.

Alfred Wegener

The Mid-Atlantic Ridge is the most famous part of the mid-ocean ridge.

The mid-ocean ridge is a huge underwater mountain range. It has a large crack running down its center. That crack is in Earth's crust. It allows molten magma to seep up. When magma reaches the surface, it is called **lava**. The lava cools and forms new rock on the ocean floor.

Rocks found near the mid-ocean ridge are younger than those that are further away. The mid-ocean ridge is pushing the sea floor of the Atlantic Ocean apart. This causes Europe and Africa to drift apart from North and South America.

Geologists had been searching for a method of continental movement. They found one in the mid-ocean ridge.

Deep and Creepy

Lots of creepy creatures lurk in the cold, murky depths of deep ocean trenches. Fangtooth fish, sea pigs, and giant tubeworms are just a few. Scientists travel many kilometers beneath the ocean's surface in tiny submarines to study these critters.

Fangtooth fish have rows of daggerlike teeth and milky-white spots where their eyes should be. Sea pigs slither along the ocean floor and munch on tasty morsels tucked into the mud. Giant tube worms flutter in breezes of superheated water. The water is heated by high temperatures within Earth's crust.

fangtooth fish

be worms

Magnetic Pole Reversal

After the mid-ocean ridge was discovered, scientists learned another thing to support plate tectonics. The rocks on the ocean floor had a **magnetic** "fingerprint."

Molten lava that comes out of the mid-ocean ridge has bits of iron in it. These molten bits line up to face the north magnetic pole. As the lava cools, the iron hardens, pointing north. But not all the iron along the ridge points north. Rocks farther away from the ridge point south. A little farther out, the iron points north again. Then another strip points south. This made scientists think that Earth's magnetic pole must be flipping. The cooled lava left a recorded fingerprint, or marker, of these flips.

The ridge widened about 2.5 centimeters (1 inch) every year. By looking at how fast the mid-ocean ridge moved apart, geologists could see the history of the flips. Earth's magnetic pole flips three or four times every million years.

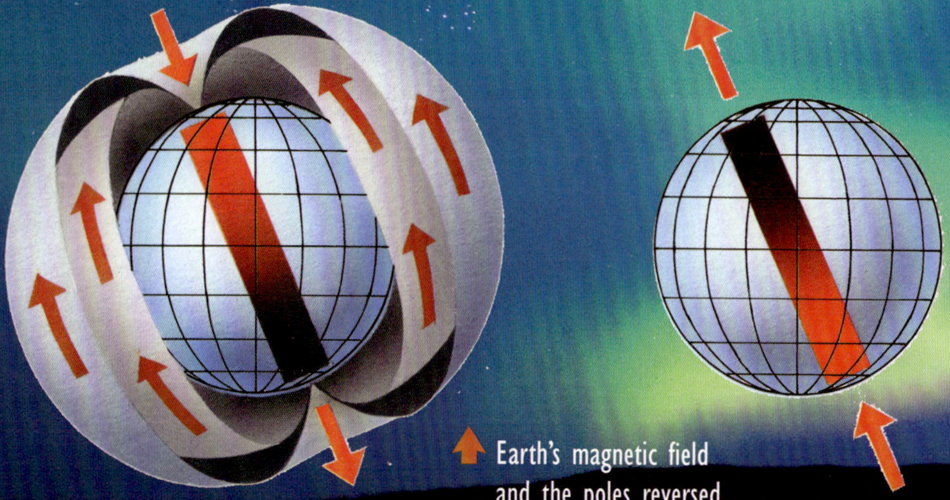

Earth's magnetic field and the poles reversed

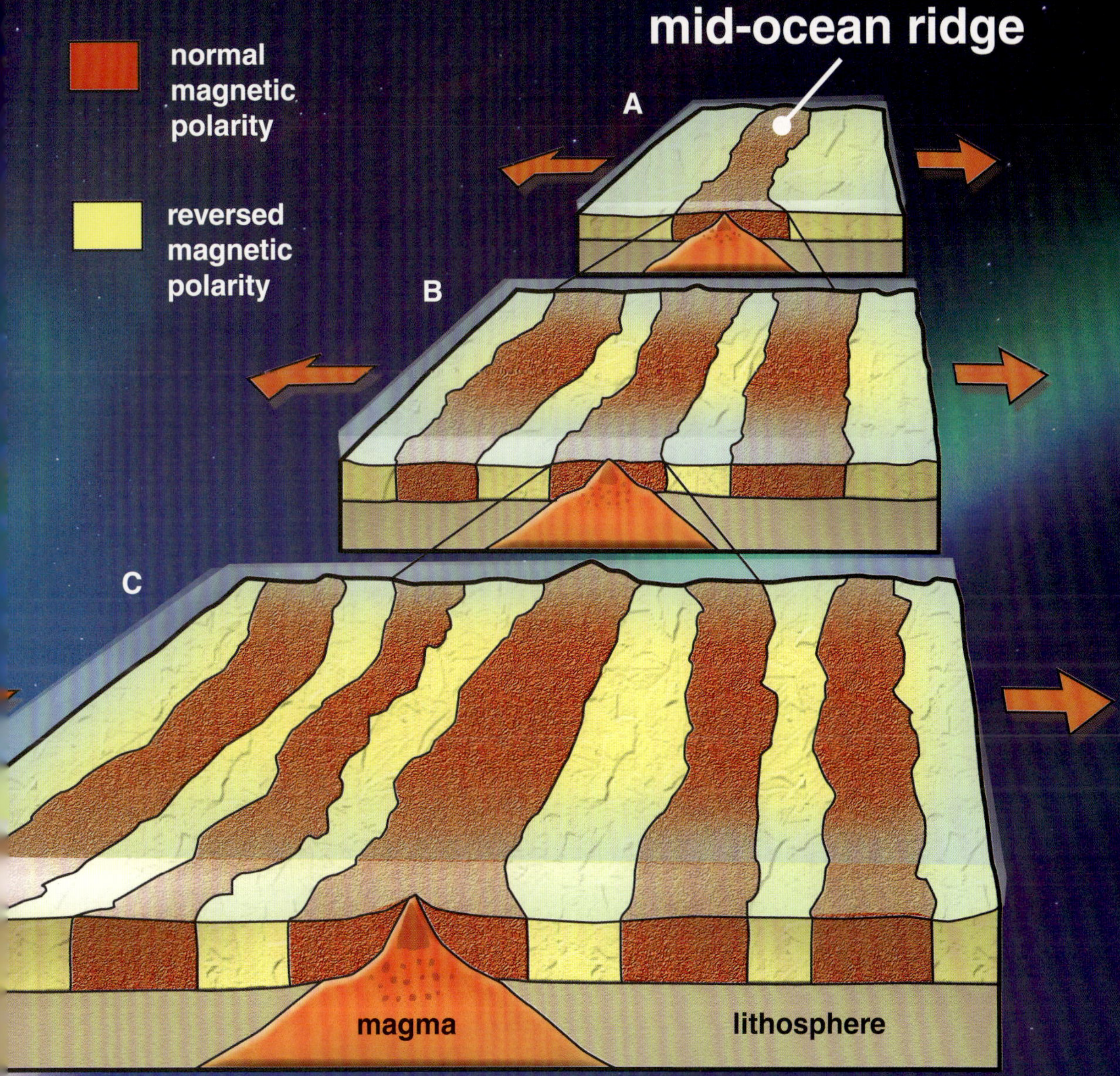

The change in Earth's magnetic field has made a pattern on the seafloor. Each time the field changes, a new stripe is made when lava flows. The change has caused a striped pattern over time.

Rocks Are Recycled

You can see how volcanoes seem to form lines across the planet. T lines are where plates collide.

Molten magma rises to the surface through cracks in Earth's crust. This makes new crust. Does that mean there is more crust on the surface of Earth now than in the past? No. Geologists had a theory. If Earth oozed molten magma in one place, then it must reabsorb crust somewhere else.

Sure enough, studies began to show that the Atlantic Ocean floor is expanding. But the Pacific Ocean floor is shrinking. It was found that the Pacific Ocean floor dives down into deep trenches under

Kilauea is an active volcano in Hawaii.

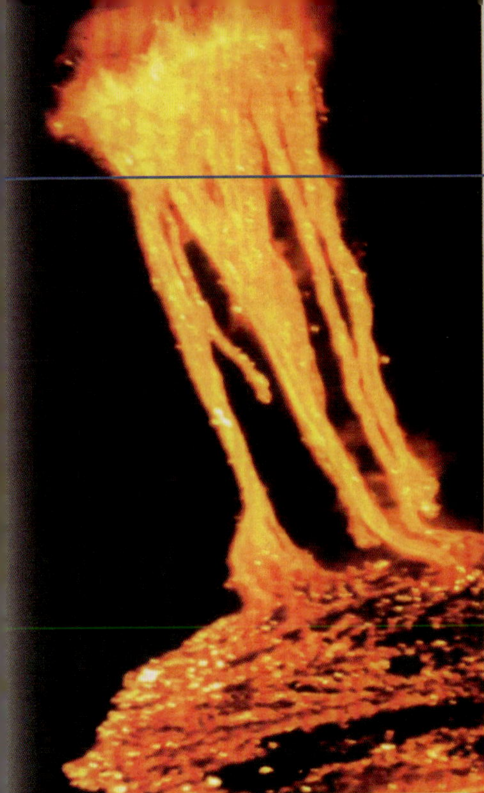

Newest Land on the Planet

Earth's surface is covered with land and ocean. But did you know that new land is being formed all the time? Every time a volcano erupts, lava flows, cools, and hardens to form new land.

Volcanoes called **seamounts** erupt deep below the surface of the ocean. Loihi is a seamount in Hawaii that will pop up sometime in the next million years! Other volcanoes like Hawaii's Kilauea belch lava. The lava burns everything in its path before steaming into the ocean to form new land.

continents. These trenches are called **subduction zones**. The expanding and shrinking ocean floors are an example of how Earth is really a recycler. Rocks are created and later recycled.

Proof of recycling rocks comes from mapping **earthquakes** and **volcanoes**. Most of them are found near undersea ridges and subduction zones.

As more and more evidence was found, Wegener became more and more respected. The theory of plate tectonics was finally accepted among scientists. Today, it is a basic part of modern geology.

Plate Boundaries

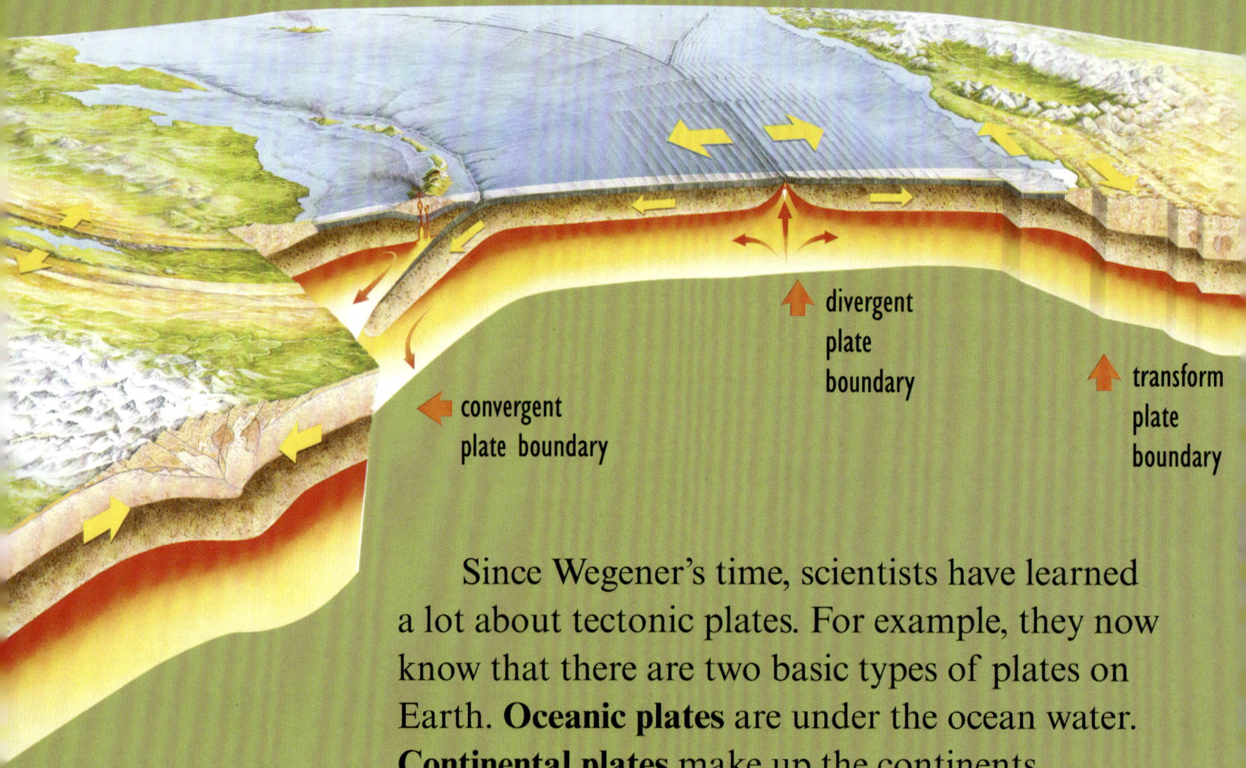

Since Wegener's time, scientists have learned a lot about tectonic plates. For example, they now know that there are two basic types of plates on Earth. **Oceanic plates** are under the ocean water. **Continental plates** make up the continents.

Scientists also know that plates have three main types of **boundaries**, or edges. They are **divergent**, **convergent**, and **transform**.

Divergent boundaries are where two plates move away from each other. Convergent boundaries are where two plates crash into each other. Transform boundaries are where two plates slide past each other.

Each boundary behaves in a different way. The different boundaries can be found all over the world. The boundaries also make land features such as mountains and valleys.

Divergent Boundaries

Iceland is a tiny island in the Atlantic Ocean. It is between Norway and Greenland. It was made from the divergent boundary of the mid-ocean ridge. Two plates are moving away from each other very slowly. They move at a rate of two to four centimeters per year.

Volcanoes are common on the island nation of Iceland. The movement of the plates causes magma to burst up and through Earth's crust. This action forms volcanoes. The cooled material from the volcanic eruptions formed Iceland.

This map shows the earth's tectonic plates and the direction each is moving.

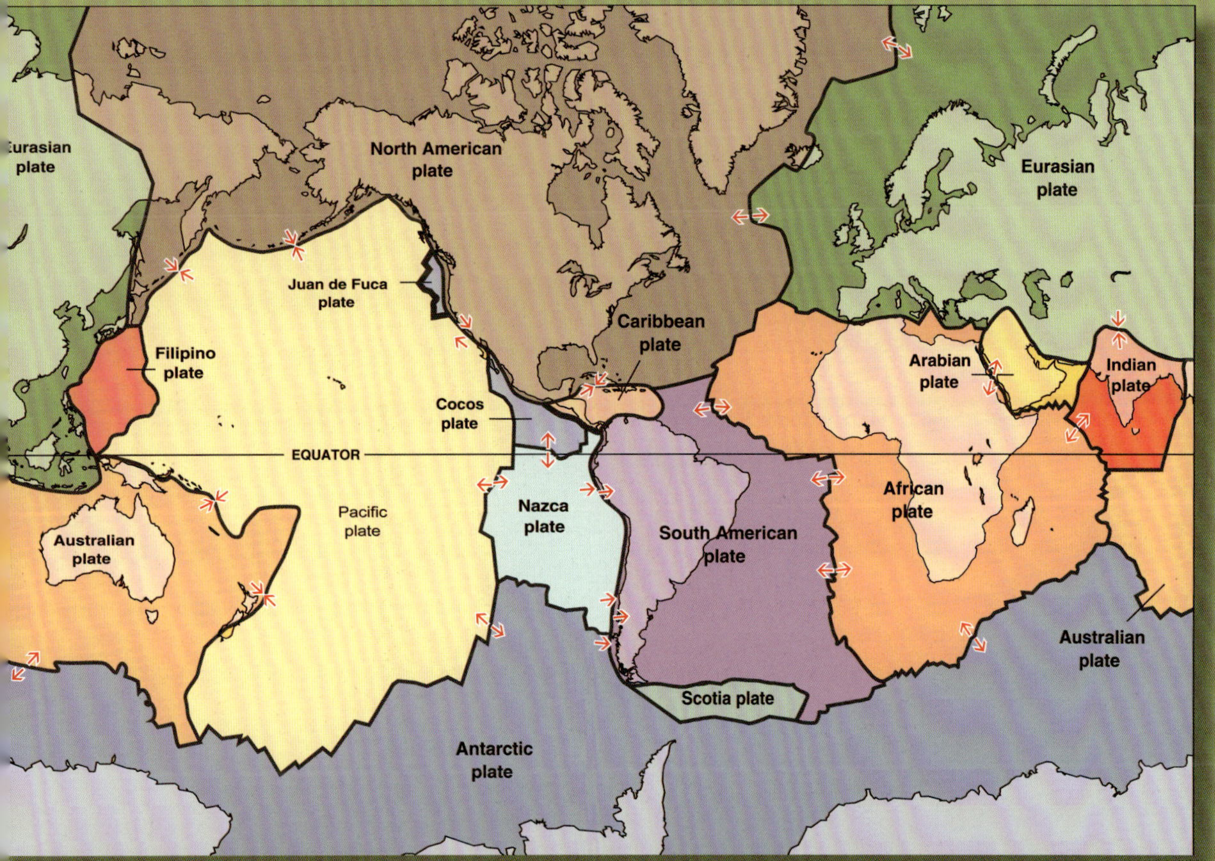

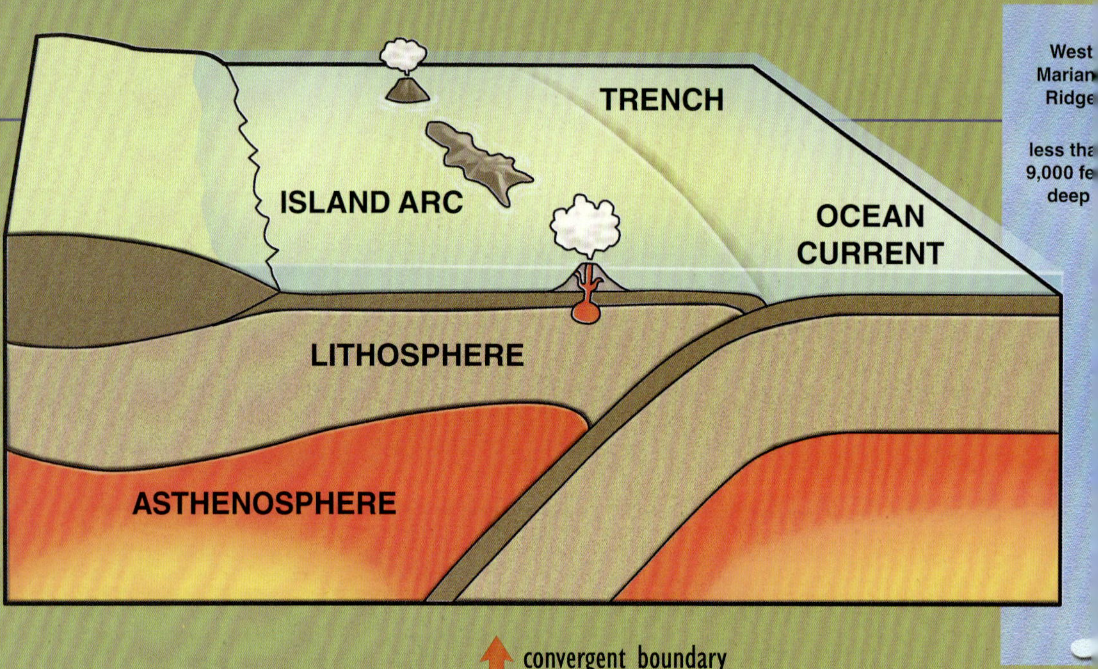

convergent boundary

Convergent Boundaries

Plates can form convergent boundaries in one of three ways. Each type of convergent boundary has its own results.

An **ocean-ocean collision** happens between two ocean plates. Right now, such a collision is causing the Mariana Trench. The fast-moving Pacific Plate is crashing into the Philippine Plate. As the Pacific Plate dives into Earth's mantle, it is melted. This causes earthquakes and volcanoes. The Mariana Islands were made in this way.

The Mariana Islands are underwater volcanoes that have grown large enough to rise above the water line. Such islands often form the shape of an arc. That is the same shape as the ocean-ocean collision boundary.

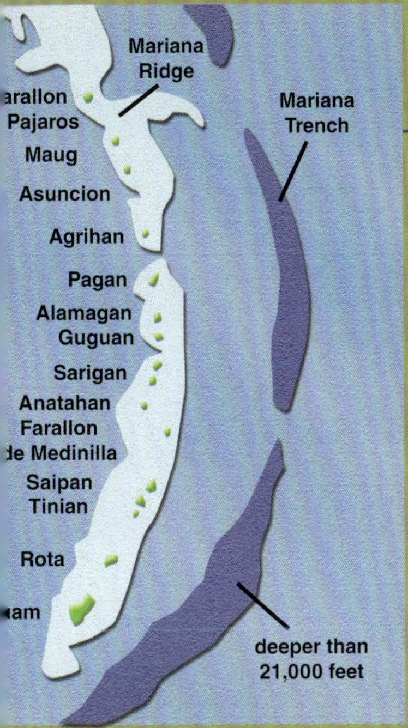

This map shows the islands that run along the same line as the ocean trench. Both were created by tectonic plates.

Tsunami!

A great tsunami hit the coast of northern Sumatra on December 26, 2004. A powerful underwater earthquake caused the tsunami. A long portion of the one plate suddenly dove under another plate. This sudden movement caused a great deal of water to be pushed outward in a circular pattern. To the east, the tsunami struck Sumatra, Indonesia, and Thailand. To the west, it struck Sri Lanka, India, and Africa.

This map shows the epicenter of a 2004 earthquake, which caused a tsunami.

An **ocean-continental collision** is happening in South America right now. An oceanic plate is being subducted under a continental plate. This is happening near Peru and Chile. That is why earthquakes and volcanoes are very common in this area of the world.

The Himalayas were created by the collision of two continental plates.

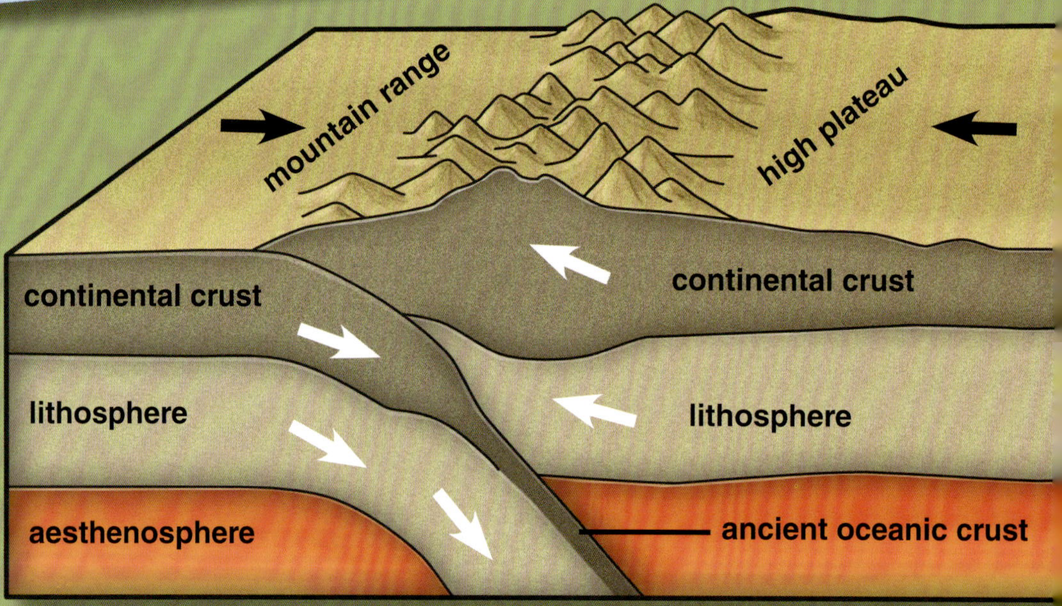

Where one plate goes on top of another, mountains are formed.

Smoking Sneakers and Real Live Lava

Imagine this. After the long trip to Volcano National Park on the island of Hawaii, you just have to see the red-hot river of lava oozing out of Kilauea. Bumpy ribbons of hardened lava are everywhere. A fiery orange streak cruises down the hillside and streams into the ocean. Billows of steam drift in the stiff breeze. As you creep along, the smell of burning rubber fills your nose. What is that smell? It's your sneakers! You don't get far before a park ranger sends you back. The ranger works hard to keep tourists safe—and their sneakers cool.

In a **continent-continent collision**, two plates collide head-on. They "fight it out" before one plate finally subducts under the other. A lot of material builds up as it is scraped off one plate before it subducts. The Himalayas are the highest mountains in the world. They are the result of a collision that started about 50 million years ago. The Indian and Eurasian continental plates crashed together to form the very tall mountain range.

Transform Boundaries

The San Andreas fault in California is a transform boundary. It falls between the Pacific Plate and the North American Plate. These two plates are sliding past each other instead of colliding into each other. This sliding motion has caused major earthquakes in California all along the state. Most transform boundaries are found in the ocean, but the San Andreas fault is on land.

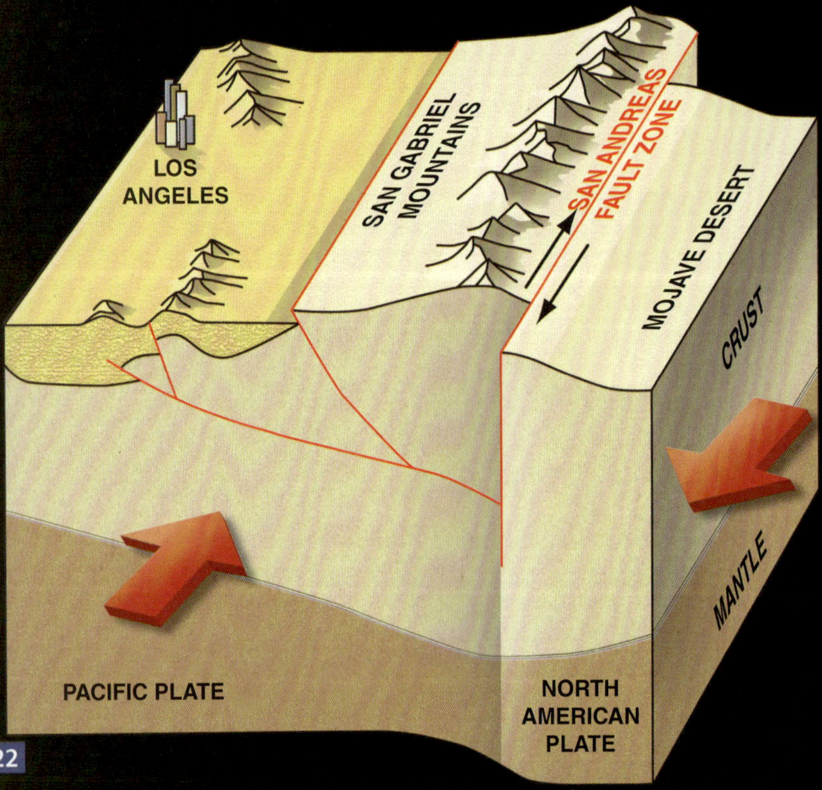

The San Andreas faultline is a transform boundary.

Aleutian Islands

The Aleutian Islands off the coast of Alaska are the result of an underwater trench. The trench has created a wide volcanic mountain range that rises above the surface of the ocean. It forms the Aleutian Islands.

Hot Spots

Some areas of the world have what are known as "hot spots." These are areas of the plates where molten magma seeps up through the crust. Imagine a hole poked in the center of a plate. That would be a hot spot. Hot spots happen in the middle of ocean plates and continental plates.

The Hawaiian Islands are an example of a hot spot in the middle of an ocean plate. The big island of Hawaii sits on top of an ancient hot spot. It has the only active volcano in the island chain. The other islands were formed when they were on top of the hot spot.

The oldest island, Kauai, is at the western end of the island chain. It has slowly moved away from the hot spot. All of the islands are on the northwestward-moving Pacific Plate. As the Pacific Plate moves, the volcanoes stop being active. They become weathered by the ocean and air.

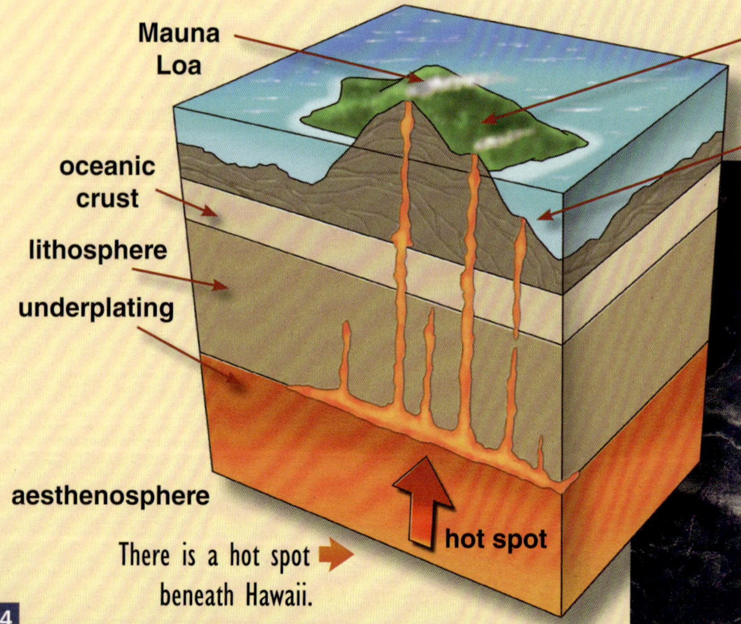

There is a hot spot beneath Hawaii.

Volcano Chasers

Some volcano scientists travel the world studying volcanoes that are about to erupt. Why? To save lives. They measure earthquakes caused by magma rumbling under Earth's surface. They also check to see if the volcano is spewing dangerous gases. They use what they find to figure out how much time there is to warn people. With enough warning, people can reach safety. In this way, scientists helped to save 20,000 lives when a volcano erupted in the Philippines.

Volcanologists sample gas coming from Mount Baker.

Each Hawaiian island was created by a hot spot's volcano before the plate moved.

This thermal pool in Yellowstone always stays warm because of the hot spot deep below it.

Yellowstone National Park is an example of a hot spot in the middle of a continental plate. The Snake River Plain in Idaho was formed when North America moved over this hot spot. The crater that Yellowstone sits in was formed after a huge volcanic eruption more than 600,000 years ago.

Earth is always changing. Plate tectonics explain a lot about how the changes happen. Earth doesn't look today the way it did millions of years ago. Earth won't look the way it does today millions of years into the future. Plate tectonics show that Earth will keep changing. Some changes will be slow. Others will be quick. One thing is for sure—as long as Earth exists, it will never be still!

The Snake River in Wyoming is on a plain formed by a hotspot.

This volcanic pool is found in Yellowstone National Park.

Lab: An "Eggsample" Look

Geologists dig deep to get an idea of what Earth looks like inside. Unfortunately, they cannot dig all the way to the core. However, geologists can use earthquakes to help them "see" inside Earth. When an earthquake happens, it sends shock waves through the planet. Earthquake waves travel differently when they pass through liquids and solids. A geologist can tell if it was solid or liquid material that the waves passed through when they receive earthquake data. By recording a number of earthquakes, geologists have a pretty good idea of what our Earth looks like inside. A core sample would be more accurate, but is not possible today. To get an idea of a core sample, try this experiment. You will drill core samples from an egg to see what it looks like inside.

Materials

- hard-boiled egg
- clear plastic drinking straw
- plastic knife
- scissors

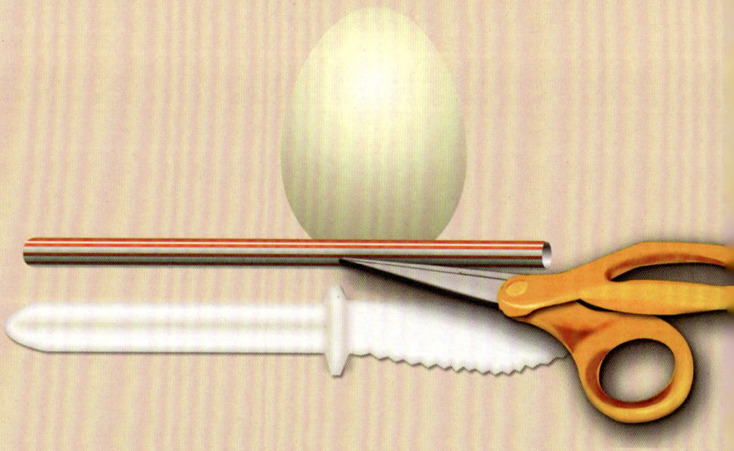

Procedure

1 Crack and peel the shell off the hard-boiled egg.

Inside Earth

2 Hold the egg in one hand and insert the straw into the top of the egg with your other hand. Slowly but firmly, press the straw through the center of the egg and out the other side.

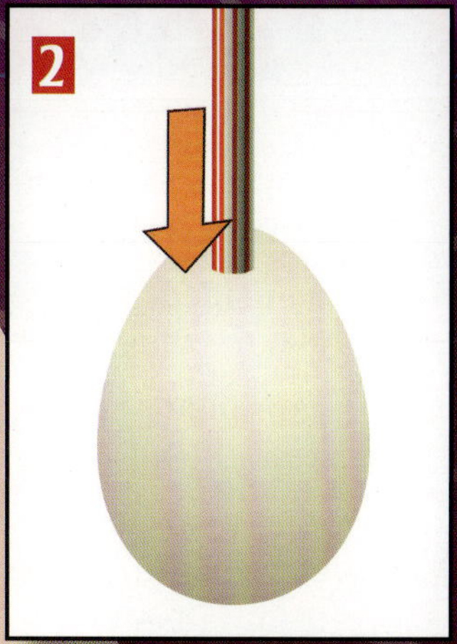

3 When the straw exits the other side of the egg, you will see parts of the egg in the straw. This is your core sample. As you continue to push, you will see a part of the straw that doesn't have any egg in it. Cut the straw at this point.

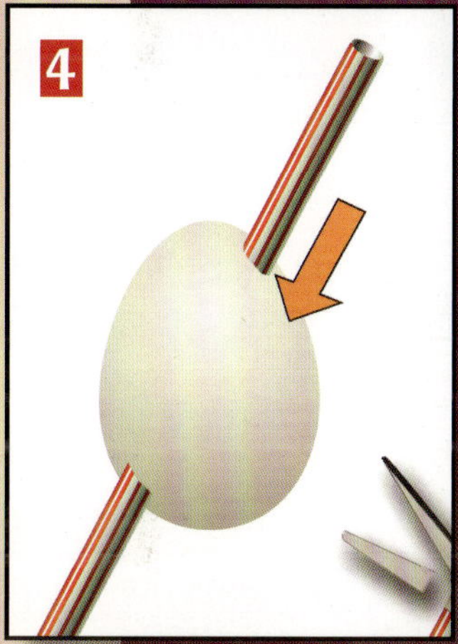

4 Pull the remaining part of the straw out of your egg. You can dig another core sample from a different location on your egg with the rest of the straw. Try entering the egg from a different angle.

5 Again, when the straw exits the egg, cut it off when you no longer see any core sample inside it.

6 Use your scissors to cut open your straw pieces. Examine your core samples.

7 Draw a picture of what you think your egg looks like inside, based on your core samples.

8 When you have drawn your picture, slice the egg open with the plastic knife to see how close your drawing is to the actual egg.

Glossary

boundaries—something that indicates a border or limit

coincidence—a remarkable series of events which have no actual connection

continent—a single large continuous area of land

continent-continent collision—two continental plates crashing into each other, producing a mountain range between them

continental drift—the idea that continents shift positions on the earth's surface

continental plates—plates that make up the continents

convergent boundaries—boundaries that occur between two plates moving toward each other

divergent boundaries—boundaries that occur between two plates moving away from each other

earthquake—a quaking, shaking, vibrating, or upheaval of Earth's surface

evidence—an available body of facts or information to help support a theory

geologist—a scientist who studies Earth's structure, substance, and history

lava—molten rock that reaches the Earth's surface

magma—hot, liquid rock

magnetic—capable of being attracted by a magnet

marine geologist–a scientist who studies Earth's oceans

mid-ocean ridge—a crack in the ocean's floor

ocean-continental collision—an oceanic plate subducting under a continental plate

ocean-ocean collision—when two ocean plates collide

oceanic plates—plates that are under the ocean

Pangea—means "all the earth"; a single land mass of all the continents put together

plate boundaries—the location where two continental plates meet

plate tectonics—the theory that Earth's crust is made up of rigid plates that float on the aesthenosphere

seamounts—an underwater mountain rising from the ocean floor but still below the surface of the water

subduction zones—an area of the earth where one plate is diving underneath another plate

submersible—a vehicle capable of operating or remaining under water

theory—a system of ideas intended to explain observations.

transform boundaries—boundaries that occur between two plates sliding past each other

trenches—a long, narrow ditch

volcano—a hill or mountain formed by the extrusion of lava or rock fragments

Index

Sally Ride Science

Sally Ride Science™ is an innovative content company dedicated to fueling young people's interests in science. Our publications and programs provide opportunities for students and teachers to explore the captivating world of science—from astrobiology to zoology. We bring science to life and show young people that science is creative, collaborative, fascinating, and fun.

Image Credits

Cover: Michael Schofield/Shutterstock; p.3 Shutterstock; p.4 (top) William A. Ceron/Shutterstock; p.4 (bottom) Bryan Busovicki/Shutterstock; p.4–5 Gary Hincks/Photo Researchers, Inc.; p.6 (background) USGS; p.6 (left) Florence Wong/USGS; p.6 (top) USGS; p.6 (right) USGS; p.7 Tim Bradley; p.8 (top) Christopher Ewing/Shutterstock; p.8–9 Tim Bradley; p.9 The Granger Collection, New York; p.10 Tim Bradley; p.11 (top) Visual&Written SL/Alamy; p.11 (bottom) Fred McConnaughey/Photo Researchers, Inc.; p.12 (top) Roman Krochuk/iStockphoto; p.12 (bottom) Gary Hincks/Photo Researchers, Inc.; p.12–13 Roman Krochuk/iStockphoto; p.14 (top) Photos.com; p.14 Tim Bradley; p.14 (center) Photos.com; p.14 (bottom) Michael Schofield/Shutterstock; p.15 (top) Photos.com; p.15 (bottom) Tim Bradley; p.16 (top) Matthew Gough/Shutterstock; p.16 Gary Hincks/Photo Researchers, Inc.; p.17 Tim Bradley; p.18 Tim Bradley; p.18–19 Tim Bradley; p.19 Tim Bradley; p.20 (top) Tim Bradley; p.20 (bottom) Tim Bradley; p.21 INTERFOTO Pressebildagentur/Alamy; p.22 Tim Bradley; p.22–23 Tim Bradley; p.23 Public Domain; p.24 (top) Shutterstock; p.24 (left) Tim Bradley; p.24 (right) NASA; p.25 (background) Time & Life Pictures/Getty Images; p.25 USGS; p.26 CAN BALCIOGLU/Shutterstock; p.27 (top) Steve Gee/iStockphoto; p.27 (bottom) Can Balcioglu/iStockphoto; p.28 (top) William A. Ceron/Shutterstock; p.28–29 Nicoll Rager Fuller